This
coloring
book belongs
to

These pages have deliberately
been left blank so that the
patterns aren't ruined due to
bleeding through from the other
side.

Also, if this book brings you
pleasure and relaxation, please
take a minute to leave a review
- it would make my day. Thanks!

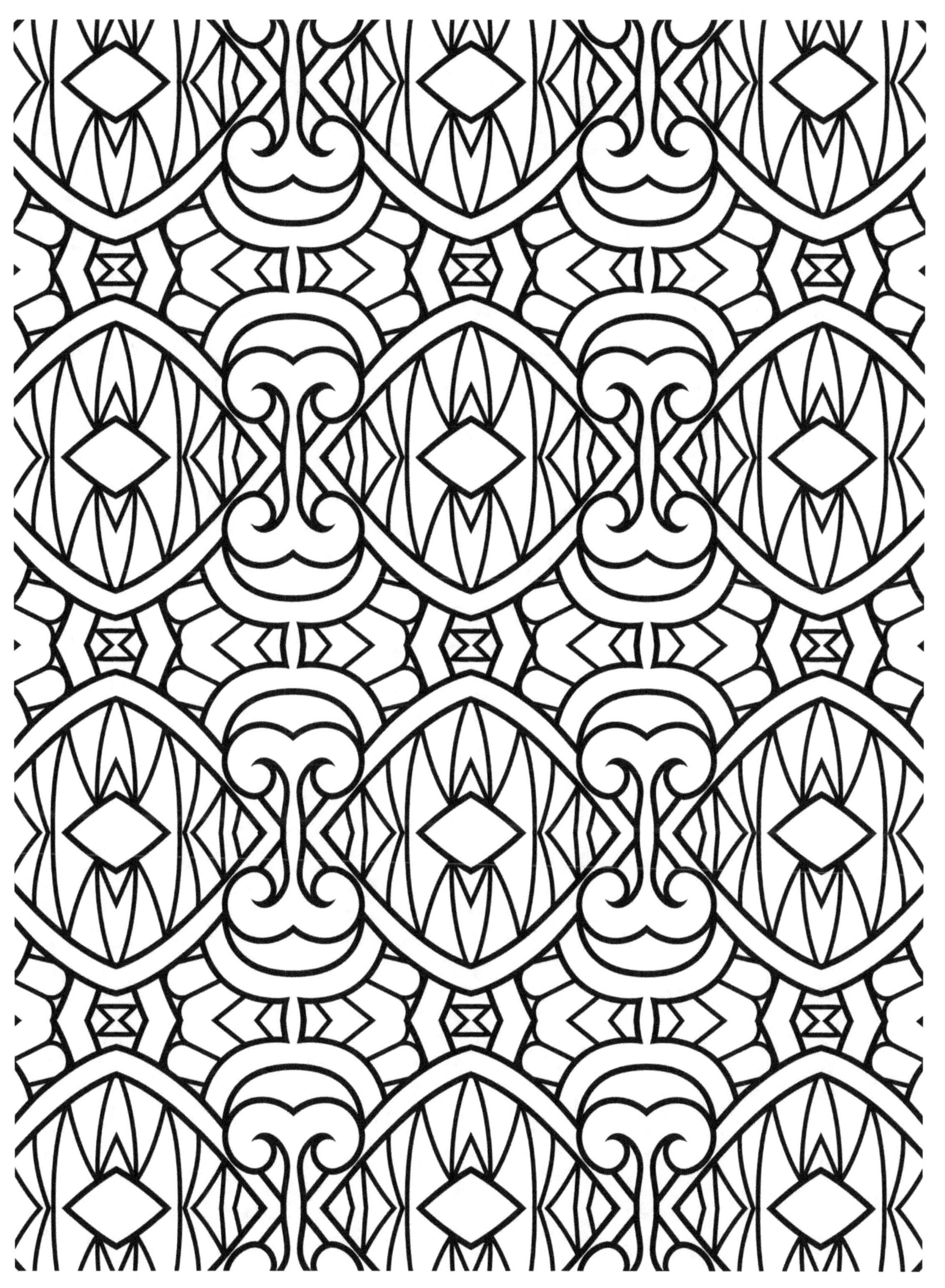